שַׁבָּת שֶׁלָּנוּ, שַׁבָּת שָׁלוֹם

Shabbat Shelanu,

Shabbat Shalom

A Family Service
for Erev Shabbat

Full-Color Edition

Rabbi Miriam Biatch
with Paul Solyn

Kikayon Publishing
Elmira, New York
www.kikayonpub.com

ISBN 978-0-615-97716-4

FOURTH PRINTING

Welcome
ברוכים הבאים, ברוכות הבאות

How do we celebrate Shabbat? שמור וזכור says Torah. We observe and we remember Shabbat. Through joy and voice, song and word, *Shabbat Shelanu, Shabbat Shalom* brings to our children a strong grounding in the ritual of our tradition while directing them into a wide flight of amazement and possibility in Jewish prayer.

Structured for children in grades 2 through 6, *Shabbat Shelanu, Shabbat Shalom* is intended to be used in a children's and family service on Friday evening. It can be introduced in Hebrew class, and it can also be used in a practice service at Hebrew school. While practicing the prayers themselves in class has great value, participating in a Shabbat service is the best way to gain the *ta'am*, the taste, of a prayerful Shabbat, and a connection to all our ancestors who have celebrated Shabbat in years past. And practicing in this way makes our Shabbat prayers simple to learn.

Our best to you for a soulful and joyous Shabbat!

Rabbi Miriam
Paul

Welcoming Shabbat

קבלת שבת

Lighting the Shabbat Candles

Ah, the Shabbat candles! The glory of the flame welcoming our Shabbat.
When we light these candles, we step into the sweetness of our Shabbat.

בָּרוּךְ אַתָּה, יְיָ, אֱלֹהֵינוּ, מֶלֶךְ הָעוֹלָם,
אֲשֶׁר קִדְּשָׁנוּ בְּמִצְוֹתָיו, וְצִוָּנוּ לְהַדְלִיק נֵר שֶׁל שַׁבָּת.

*Barukh Atah, Adonai, Eloheinu melekh ha-olam, asher kid'shanu
b'mitzvotav, v'tzivanu l'hadlik neir shel Shabbat.*

We praise You, Adonai our God.
You taught us to light these lights for Shabbat.

Opening Songs

Shalom Aleichem

שָׁלוֹם עֲלֵיכֶם, מַלְאֲכֵי הַשָּׁרֵת,
מַלְאֲכֵי עֶלְיוֹן,
מִמֶּלֶךְ מַלְכֵי הַמְּלָכִים,
הַקָּדוֹשׁ בָּרוּךְ הוּא.

בּוֹאֲכֶם לְשָׁלוֹם, מַלְאֲכֵי הַשָּׁלוֹם,
מַלְאֲכֵי עֶלְיוֹן,
מִמֶּלֶךְ מַלְכֵי הַמְּלָכִים,
הַקָּדוֹשׁ בָּרוּךְ הוּא.

בָּרְכוּנִי לְשָׁלוֹם, מַלְאֲכֵי הַשָּׁלוֹם,
מַלְאֲכֵי עֶלְיוֹן,
מִמֶּלֶךְ מַלְכֵי הַמְּלָכִים,
הַקָּדוֹשׁ בָּרוּךְ הוּא.

צֵאתְכֶם לְשָׁלוֹם, מַלְאֲכֵי הַשָּׁלוֹם,
מַלְאֲכֵי עֶלְיוֹן,
מִמֶּלֶךְ מַלְכֵי הַמְּלָכִים,
הַקָּדוֹשׁ בָּרוּךְ הוּא.

Shalom aleikhem, malakhei ha-shareit, malakhei elyon,
mimelekh mal'khei ha-m'lakhim, ha-kadosh barukh hu.

Bo'akhem l'shalom, malakhei ha-shalom, malakhei elyon,
mimelekh mal'khei ha-m'lakhim, ha-kadosh barukh hu.

Bar'khuni l'shalom, malakhei ha-shalom, malakhei elyon,
mimelekh mal'khei ha-m'lakhim, ha-kadosh barukh hu.

Tzeit'khem l'shalom, malakhei ha-shalom, malakhei elyon,
mimelekh mal'khei ha-m'lakhim, ha-kadosh barukh hu.

Shabbat has come and the messengers of Adonai bringing us her blessings.

Shabbat has come and we enter with wholeness and joy.

Shabbat has come to stay only a short time, and then she will depart, only to arrive in a short while, with the messengers of Adonai bringing her to us once again.

לְכָה דוֹדִי לִקְרַאת כַּלָּה, פְּנֵי שַׁבָּת נְקַבְּלָה.

שָׁמוֹר וְזָכוֹר בְּדִבּוּר אֶחָד,
הִשְׁמִיעָנוּ אֵל הַמְיֻחָד,
יְיָ אֶחָד וּשְׁמוֹ אֶחָד,
לְשֵׁם וּלְתִפְאֶרֶת וְלִתְהִלָּה.

לִקְרַאת שַׁבָּת לְכוּ וְנֵלְכָה,
כִּי הִיא מְקוֹר הַבְּרָכָה,
מֵרֹאשׁ מִקֶּדֶם נְסוּכָה,
סוֹף מַעֲשֶׂה בְּמַחֲשָׁבָה תְּחִלָּה.

הִתְעוֹרְרִי, הִתְעוֹרְרִי,
כִּי בָא אוֹרֵךְ, קוּמִי אוֹרִי,
עוּרִי עוּרִי, שִׁיר דַּבֵּרִי,
כְּבוֹד יְיָ עָלַיִךְ נִגְלָה.

בּוֹאִי בְשָׁלוֹם עֲטֶרֶת בַּעְלָהּ,
גַּם בְּשִׂמְחָה וּבְצָהֳלָה,
תּוֹךְ אֱמוּנֵי עַם סְגֻלָּה,
בּוֹאִי כַלָּה, בּוֹאִי כַלָּה.

L'cha dodi, likrat kallah, p'nei shabbat n'kab'lah.

Shamor v'zachor b'dibur echad,
hishmianu eil ha-m'yuchad,
Adonai echad u-sh'mo echad,
l'sheim ul-tiferet v'lit-hilah.

Likrat shabbat l'khu v'neilkhah,
ki hi m'kor ha-b'rakhah,
meirosh mikedem n'sukhah,
sof ma'aseh b'machashavah t'chilah.

Hit'or'ri, hit'or'ri,
ki va oreikh kumi ori,
uri, uri, shir dabeiri,
k'vod Adonai alayikh niglah.

Bo'i v'shalom ateret ba'lah,
gam b'simkhah u-v'tzoholah,
tokh emunei am s'gulah,
bo'i khallah, bo'i khallah.

Let us go out to meet Shabbat, our bride, our queen,
for when we greet her, we greet our God.
Let us go out to meet Shabbat, Shabbat that is like a fountain
of blessings, like waters for play and for joy.
It's Shabbat, wake up and sing, welcome the bride, our queen, and our Shabbat.

Sh'ma and Its Blessings

שמע וברכותיה

בָּרְכוּ אֶת יהוה הַמְבֹרָךְ.

בָּרוּךְ יהוה הַמְבֹרָךְ לְעוֹלָם וָעֶד.

Ba-r'chu et Adonai ham'vorach.
Baruch Adonai ham'vorach l'olam va'ed.

We praise You, Adonai, for You are praiseworthy!

We praise You, Adonai, for You are praiseworthy forever and ever!

The Bringer of the Night

מעריב ערבים

בָּרוּךְ אַתָּה יהוה אֱלֹהֵנוּ מֶלֶךְ הָעוֹלָם אֲשֶׁר בִּדְבָרוֹ מַעֲרִיב
עֲרָבִים, בְּחָכְמָה פּוֹתֵחַ שְׁעָרִים, וּבִתְבוּנָה מְשַׁנֶּה עִתִּים, וּמַחֲלִיף
אֶת-הַזְּמַנִּים, וּמְסַדֵּר אֶת-הַכּוֹכָבִים בְּמִשְׁמְרוֹתֵהֶם בָּרָקִיעַ
כִּרְצוֹנוֹ. בּוֹרֵא יוֹם וָלַיְלָה, גּוֹלֵל אוֹר מִפְּנֵי חֹשֶׁךְ וְחֹשֶׁךְ מִפְּנֵי
אוֹר, וּמַעֲבִיר יוֹם וּמֵבִיא לַיְלָה, וּמַבְדִּיל בֵּין יוֹם וּבֵין לַיְלָה, יי
צְבָאוֹת שְׁמוֹ. אֵל חַי וְקַיָּם תָּמִיד יִמְלוֹךְ עָלֵינוּ, לְעוֹלָם וָעֶד.

Barukh atah Adonai Eloheinu melekh ha-olam, asher bidvaro ma'ariv aravim,
b'chokhmah poteiach sh'arim, u-vitvunah m'shaneh itim, u-machalif et ha-z'manim,
u-m'sader et-hakokhavim b'mish-m'roteihem barakiya kirtzono.
Borei yom valailah, goleil or mip'nei choshekh v'choshekh mip'nei or,
u-ma'avir yom u-meivi lailah, u-mavdil bein yom u-vein lailah, Adonai tz'va-ot sh'mo.
Eil chai v'kayam tamid yimlokh aleinu l'olam va-ed.

We praise You, Adonai. By just Your words
You bring the evening to us.
You are wise beyond wise.
You make time go by.
You move the seasons from summer to autumn,
and from winter to spring.
You set the stars in the sky,
and they make pictures for us to see.
You make day and night,
by making the world go around and around,
and we can depend on You.
We are glad you are our God!

בָּרוּךְ אַתָּה יְיָ,
הַמַּעֲרִיב עֲרָבִים.

Baruch Atah Adonai, ha-ma'ariv aravim.

**We praise You, Adonai, you are
the Bringer of the night.**

The One Who Loves the People Israel
אהבת עולם

אַהֲבַת עוֹלָם בֵּית יִשְׂרָאֵל עַמְּךָ אָהַבְתָּ.

תּוֹרָה וּמִצְוֹת, חֻקִּים וּמִשְׁפָּטִים אוֹתָנוּ לִמַּדְתָּ.

עַל־כֵּן יהוה אֱלֹהֵינוּ בְּשָׁכְבֵּנוּ וּבְקוּמֵנוּ נָשִׂיחַ בְּחֻקֶּיךָ,

וְנִשְׂמַח בְּדִבְרֵי תוֹרָתֶךָ וּבְמִצְוֹתֶיךָ לְעוֹלָם וָעֶד.

כִּי הֵם חַיֵּינוּ וְאֹרֶךְ יָמֵינוּ וּבָהֶם נֶהְגֶּה יוֹמָם וָלָיְלָה.

וְאַהֲבָתְךָ אַל־תָּסִיר מִמֶּנּוּ לְעוֹלָמִים!

Ahavat olam beit yisrael, amkha ahav'ta
Torah u-mitzvot chukim u-mishpatim, otanu l'madta.
Al kein Adonai Eloheinu, b'shokhbaynu u-v'kumaynu nasiach b'chukekha.
V'nismakh b'divrei toratekha,
u-v'mitzvotekha l'olam va'ed.
Ki heim chayeinu v'orekh yameinu
u-vahem neh-geh yomam va'lailah.
V'ahavatkha al tasir mimenu l'olamim.
Barukh Atah Adonai oheiv amo yisrael.

You have loved us, Your people, the House of Israel, from the start, and You gave us Torah. What a gift!

When we read Your Torah, we learn Your laws and Your Mitzvot.

And then, at night and in the morning we sing about who we are as Jews. Then we know that we will always feel You in our hearts.

בָּרוּךְ אַתָּה יהוה אוֹהֵב עַמּוֹ יִשְׂרָאֵל.

Barukh Atah Adonai, ohev amo yisrael.

Blessed are You, Adonai. You love us, Your people Israel.

Hear, O Israel!

שְׁמַע יִשְׂרָאֵל יהוה אֱלֹהֵינוּ יהוה אֶחָד.
בָּרוּךְ שֵׁם כְּבוֹד מַלְכוּתוֹ לְעוֹלָם וָעֶד.

Sh'ma Yisrael Adonai Eloheinu Adonai echad.

Barukh sheim k'vod malkhuto l'olam va'ed.

What is that we hear:
That Adonai is our God, and Adonai is our only God!

And we praise Adonai for ever and ever.

And You Shall Love Adonai

וְאָהַבְתָּ אֵת יהוה אֱלֹהֶיךָ בְּכָל-לְבָבְךָ וּבְכָל-נַפְשְׁךָ וּבְכָל-מְאֹדֶךָ.
וְהָיוּ הַדְּבָרִים הָאֵלֶּה, אֲשֶׁר אָנֹכִי מְצַוְּךָ הַיּוֹם, עַל לְבָבֶךָ.
וְשִׁנַּנְתָּם לְבָנֶיךָ, וְדִבַּרְתָּ בָּם, בְּשִׁבְתְּךָ בְּבֵיתֶךָ, וּבְלֶכְתְּךָ בַדֶּרֶךְ,
וּבְשָׁכְבְּךָ וּבְקוּמֶךָ. וּקְשַׁרְתָּם לְאוֹת עַל-יָדֶךָ, וְהָיוּ לְטֹטָפֹת בֵּין
עֵינֶיךָ, וּכְתַבְתָּם עַל-מְזֻזוֹת בֵּיתֶךָ וּבִשְׁעָרֶיךָ.

לְמַעַן תִּזְכְּרוּ וַעֲשִׂיתֶם אֶת-כָּל-מִצְוֹתָי וִהְיִיתֶם קְדֹשִׁים
לֵאלֹהֵיכֶם. אֲנִי יהוה אֱלֹהֵיכֶם אֲשֶׁר הוֹצֵאתִי אֶתְכֶם מֵאֶרֶץ
מִצְרַיִם לִהְיוֹת לָכֶם לֵאלֹהִים. אֲנִי יהוה אֱלֹהֵיכֶם.

V'ahavta eit Adonai Elohekha,
b'khol levav'kha uv'khol nafshekha, uv'khol m'odekha. V'hayu hadvarim
ha'eyleh asher anokhi mitzav'kha hayom al l'vavekha.
V'shinantam l'vanekha v'dibarta bam,
b'shivt'kha b'veitecha uv'lekh't'kha vaderech uv'shakh'b'kha uv'kumekha.
Uk'shartam l'ot al yadekha, v'hayu l'totafot bein einekha.
Ukh'tavtem al mezuzot beitekha u-vish'arekha. L'ma'an tiz-k'ru va'asitem et-kol-
mitzvotai, vi-h'yitem k'doshim leiloheikhem. Ani Adonai Eloheikhem
asher hotzeiti etkhem mei'eretz mitzrayim
lih'yot lakhem leilohim. Ani Adonai Eloheikhem.

This is what our teachers tell us:
when we learn the words of Torah, they start to live in your heart.
When we have children of our own, we can teach them these words;
we can talk about these words
even today to our mothers and fathers;
when we are out of the house or inside;
when we are in bed, or when we arise,
and even when we are in the car.
We can put them into a mezuzah,
so that we can see the words when we go through a door.
These are great words! They teach about being a Jew!

Who Is Like Adonai?

מִי־כָמֹכָה בָּאֵלִם יהוה?

מִי כָּמֹכָה נֶאְדָּר בַּקֹּדֶשׁ,

נוֹרָא תְהִלֹּת, עֹשֵׂה פֶלֶא?

מַלְכוּתְךָ רָאוּ בָנֶיךָ, בּוֹקֵעַ יָם לִפְנֵי מֹשֶׁה,

זֶה אֵלִי! עָנוּ וְאָמְרוּ:

יהוה יִמְלֹךְ לְעֹלָם וָעֶד.

Mi Khamokha ba'eilim Adonai,
mi kamokha ne'dar bakodesh,
norah t'hilot oseh feleh?
Malkhut'cha ra'u vanekha bokei'a yam
lifnei Moshe,
zeh eili anu v'amru:
Adonai yimlokh l'olam va'ed.

Who is like You, Adonai?
Who is like You, so great,
and far from us, and yet so near
that we each can speak to You
in our own ways?
What a wonder!

Shelter of Peace

הַשְׁכִּיבֵנוּ, יְיָ אֱלוֹהֵנוּ, לְשָׁלוֹם,

וְהַעֲמִידֵנוּ שׁוֹמְרֵנוּ לְחַיִּים,

וּפְרֹשׂ עָלֵינוּ סֻכַּת שְׁלוֹמֶךָ,

וְתַקְּנֵנוּ בְּעֵצָה טוֹבָה מִלְּפָנֶךָ,

וְהוֹשִׁיעֵנוּ לְמַעַן שְׁמֶךָ,

וְהָגֵן בַּעֲדֵנוּ,

וְהָסֵר מֵעָלֵינוּ אוֹרֵב, דֶּבֶר,

וְחֶרֶב, וְרָעָב, וְיָגוֹן,

וְהַרְחֵק מִמֶּנּוּ עָוֹן וָפֶשַׁע.

וּבְצֵל כְּנָפֶיךָ תַּסְתִּירֵנוּ,

כִּי אֵל שׁוֹמְרֵנוּ וּמַצִּילֵנוּ אָתָּה,

כִּי אֵל חַנּוּן וְרַחוּם אָתָּה.

וּשְׁמֹר צֵאתֵנוּ וּבוֹאֵנוּ לְחַיִּים וּלְשָׁלוֹם

מֵעַתָּה וְעַד עוֹלָם.

Hashkiveinu, Adonai Eloheinu, l'shalom, v'ha-amideinu shom'reinu l'chayyim, u-f'ros aleinu sukkat sh'lomekha, v'tak'neinu b'eitzah tovah mil'fanekha, v'hoshi'einu l'ma'an sh'mekha, v'hagein ba'adeinu, v'haser mei'aleinu oreiv, dever, v'cherev, v'ra'av, v'yagor, v'ha-r'cheik mimenu avon vafesha. U-v'tzeil k'nafekha tastireinu, ki Eil shomreinu u-matzileinu Atah, ki Eil chanun v'rachum Atah. U-sh'mor tzeiteinu u-vo'einu l'chayyim u-l'shalom mei'atah v'ad olam.

Deep in our hearts, our Shabbat prayer asks that we find rest when we sleep, and strength when we are awake. We pray that war will cease, that everyone will have food to eat, a place to sleep, and people to love. This is our Shabbat prayer.

בָּרוּךְ אַתָּה יְיָ,
הַפּוֹרֵשׁ סֻכַּת שָׁלוֹם עָלֵינוּ
וְעַל כָּל עַמּוֹ יִשְׂרָאֵל וְעַל יְרוּשָׁלָיִם.

Barukh Atah Adonai, haporeis sukkat shalom aleinu v'al kol amo yisrael v'al y'rushalayim.

We praise You, Adonai. You spread a shelter of peace over us, over all Your people Israel, and over Jerusalem.

You Shall Keep Shabbat

וְשָׁמְרוּ בְנֵי יִשְׂרָאֵל אֶת־הַשַּׁבָּת,
לַעֲשׂוֹת אֶת־הַשַּׁבָּת לְדֹרֹתָם
בְּרִית עוֹלָם.
בֵּינִי וּבֵין בְּנֵי יִשְׂרָאֵל
אוֹת הִיא לְעוֹלָם,
כִּי־שֵׁשֶׁת יָמִים עָשָׂה יְיָ
אֶת־הַשָּׁמַיִם וְאֶת־הָאָרֶץ,
וּבַיּוֹם הַשְּׁבִיעִי שָׁבַת וַיִּנָּפַשׁ.

V'shamru v'nei yisrael et ha-shabbat, la'asot et ha-shabbat l'dorotam, b'rit olam.
Beini u-vein b'nei yisrael ot hi l'olam, ki sheshet yamim asah Adonai et
ha-shamayim v'et ha'aretz, u-vayom ha-sh'vi'i shavat vayinafash.

Shabbat is a grand day for rest. We have celebrated Shabbat for years and years, since the beginning of time, since Adonai made the heaven and the earth, and Adonai rested. We can do that too. Let's do that together!

T'filah

תפלה

Open Our Lips

אֲדֹנָי, שְׂפָתַי תִּפְתָּח, וּפִי יַגִּיד תְּהִלָּתֶךָ.

Adonai, s'fatai tiftach, u-fi yagid t'hilatekha.

Adonai, open up our lips, so our mouths may declare Your praise.

Adonai, when we pray, Your words are on paper, but they become holy when they flow out of our mouths. We thank you for our lips, and we praise You.

God of Our Ancestors

אבות ואמהות

בָּרוּךְ אַתָּה יהוה אֱלֹהֵינוּ וֵאלֹהֵי אֲבוֹתֵינוּ וְאִמּוֹתֵינוּ,

אֱלֹהֵי אַבְרָהָם, אֱלֹהֵי יִצְחָק, וֵאלֹהֵי יַעֲקֹב.

אֱלֹהֵי שָׂרָה, אֱלֹהֵי רִבְקָה, אֱלֹהֵי לֵאָה, וֵאלֹהֵי רָחֵל.

הָאֵל הַגָּדוֹל הַגִּבּוֹר וְהַנּוֹרָא אֵל עֶלְיוֹן,

גּוֹמֵל חֲסָדִים טוֹבִים, וְקוֹנֵה הַכֹּל, וְזוֹכֵר חַסְדֵי אָבוֹת וְאִמָּהוֹת,

וּמֵבִיא גְאֻלָּה לִבְנֵי בְנֵיהֶם, לְמַעַן שְׁמוֹ בְּאַהֲבָה.

מֶלֶךְ עוֹזֵר וּמוֹשִׁיעַ וּמָגֵן.

בָּרוּךְ אַתָּה יהוה מָגֵן אַבְרָהָם וְעֶזְרַת שָׂרָה.

Barukh Atah Adonai Eloheinu veilohei avoteinu v'imoteinu, elohei avraham, elohei
yitzchak, veilohei ya'akov, eilohei sarah, eilohei rikvah eilohei leah, veilohei rachel,
ha-eil ha-gadol ha-gibor v'hanorah eil elyon.
Gomeil chasadim tovim, v'konei hakol v'zokheir chasdei avot v'imahot
u'meivi g'ulah livnei v'neihem l'ma'an shemo b'ahavah.
Melekh ozeir u'moshia umagein.
Barukh Atah Adonai magein Avraham v'ezrat Sarah.

We praise you Adonai, our God!
You are the God of all
our fathers and our mothers
who lived long ago:
You're the God of Abraham, God of Isaac, and God of Jacob;
You're the God of Sarah, God of Rebekah, God of Leah,
and God of Rachel.

All of our ancestors were loyal to You,
and like them,
we will be loyal to You.
We praise You, Adonai our God,
You are the God
and protector of our People Israel.

God's Strength

גבורות

אַתָּה גִבּוֹר לְעוֹלָם אֲדֹנָי, מְחַיֵּה הַכֹּל אַתָּה, רַב לְהוֹשִׁיעַ.

מְכַלְכֵּל חַיִּים בְּחֶסֶד, מְחַיֵּה הַכֹּל בְּרַחֲמִים רַבִּים,

סוֹמֵךְ נוֹפְלִים, וְרוֹפֵא חוֹלִים וּמַתִּיר אֲסוּרִים,

וּמְקַיֵּם אֱמוּנָתוֹ לִישֵׁנֵי עָפָר.

מִי כָמוֹךָ בַּעַל גְּבוּרוֹת, וּמִי דּוֹמֶה לָּךְ,

מֶלֶךְ מֵמִית וּמְחַיֶּה וּמַצְמִיחַ יְשׁוּעָה.

וְנֶאֱמָן אַתָּה לְהַחֲיוֹת הַכֹּל. בָּרוּךְ אַתָּה יהוה מְחַיֵּה הַכֹּל.

Atah gibor l'olam Adonai, m'chayei hakol Atah, rav l'hoshia.
M'khal-keil chayim b'chesed, m'chayei hakol b'rachamim rabim.
Someikh nof'lim v'rofei cholim, umatir asurim, u'mikayeim emunato, lisheinei afar.
Mi khamokha ba'al g'vurot, umi domeh lakh.
Melekh meimit u-m'chayei umatzmiach yeshuah.
Vene'eman Atah l'hachayot hakol. Barukh Atah Adonai michayei hakol.

Adonai our God,
all life is Your gift to us!
You are happy
when we feel good;
and Your arms are around us
when we feel bad.
You remind us
to help people who fall down,
and Your Torah tells us
to help people who are sick.
You remind us that freedom
is the most important thing
for everyone in the world,
and we must work for freedom everyday.
We praise You, Adonai.
You are so strong for us all.

God's Holiness

קדושת השם

אַתָּה קָדוֹשׁ וְשִׁמְךָ קָדוֹשׁ וּקְדוֹשִׁים בְּכָל יוֹם יְהַלְלוּךָ סֶּלָה.
בָּרוּךְ אַתָּה יהוה הָאֵל הַקָּדוֹשׁ.

Atah kadosh, v'shimkha kadosh, u-k'doshim b'khol yom y'hal'lukha selah.
Barukh Atah Adonai ha-eil hakadosh.

You are holy and special,
and Your name is holy and special;
and we, who try to be holy and special,
are happy that we're like You!
We praise You, Adonai, the holy God.

Accept Our Prayer

רְצֵה, יְיָ אֱלֹהֵינוּ, בְּעַמְּךָ יִשְׂרָאֵל, וּתְפִלָּתָם בְּאַהֲבָה תְקַבֵּל,
וּתְהִי לְרָצוֹן תָּמִיד עֲבוֹדַת יִשְׂרָאֵל עַמֶּךָ.
אֵל קָרוֹב לְכָל קֹרְאָיו, פְּנֵה אֶל עֲבָדֶךָ וְחָנֵּנוּ,
שְׁפוֹךְ רוּחֲךָ עָלֵינוּ.

R'tzei, Adonai Eloheinu, b'am'kha yisrael, u-t'filatam b'ahavah t'kabeil,
u-t'hi l'ratzon tamid avodat yisrael amekha.
Eil karov l'khol kor'av, p'nei el avdekha v'chaneinu,
sh'fokh ruchakha aleinu.

Adonai, Your world is a wonderful place! And we pray that
You hear everything we pray and smile upon us.

Overflowing Peace
שלום רב

שָׁלוֹם רָב עַל־יִשְׂרָאֵל עַמְּךָ תָּשִׂים לְעוֹלָם,

כִּי אַתָּה הוּא מֶלֶךְ אָדוֹן לְכָל הַשָּׁלוֹם.

וְטוֹב בְּעֵינֶיךָ לְבָרֵךְ אֶת־עַמְּךָ יִשְׂרָאֵל,

בְּכָל־עֵת וּבְכָל־שָׁעָה בִּשְׁלוֹמֶךָ.

Shalom rav al yisrael amkha tasim l'olam.
Ki Atah hu melech adon, l'khol ha-shalom.
V'tov b'einekha l'vareikh et am'kha yisrael, b'khol eit u-v'khol sha'ah bishlomekha.

Adonai, our God, we hope to help You bring peace over Israel forever.
We Praise You, Adonai, You help us find strength to
help Israel and all the world find peace.

בָּרוּךְ אַתָּה יהוה

הַמְבָרֵךְ אֶת עַמּוֹ יִשְׂרָאֵל בַּשָּׁלוֹם.

Barukh Atah Adonai hamvareikh et amo yisrael bashalom.

Prayer of the Heart

תפלת הלב

*Let's make our own personal
and quiet prayer.*

Let Us Make Peace

עושה שלום

עֹשֶׂה שָׁלוֹם בִּמְרוֹמָיו הוּא יַעֲשֶׂה שָׁלוֹם עָלֵינוּ
וְעַל־כָּל־יִשְׂרָאֵל, וְאִמְרוּ אָמֵן.

Oseh shalom bimromav hu ya'aseh shalom, aleinu
v'al kol yisrael, v'imru amein.

May Adonai who brings
peace to all the universe,
help us make peace among ourselves
and all the world,
and let us all say: Amen.

Prayer for Healing

מי שברך

מִי שֶׁבֵּרַךְ אֲבוֹתֵנוּ וְאִמוֹתֵנוּ, אַבְרָהָם וְשָׂרָה, יִצְחָק וְרִבְקָה, יַעֲקֹב
וְרָחֵל וְלֵאָה, הוּא יְבָרֵךְ אֶת הַחוֹלִים. הַקָדוֹשׁ בָּרוּךְ הוּא יְמַלֵא
רַחֲמִים עֲלֵיהֶם, לְהַחֲלִימָם וּלְרַפֹּאתָם וּלְהַחֲזִיקָם, וְיִשְׁלַח לָהֶם
מְהֵרָה רְפוּאָה שְׁלֵמָה מִן הַשָּׁמַיִם, רְפוּאַת הַנֶּפֶשׁ וּרְפוּאַת הַגוּף,
הַשְׁתָּא בַּעֲגָלָה וּבִזְמַן קָרִיב. וְנֹאמַר: אָמֵן.

*Mi shebeirakh avoteinu v'imoteinu, Avraham v'Sarah, Yitzchak v'Rivkah, Ya'akov v'Racheil v'Leah,
Hu y'vareikh et ha-cholim. Ha-kadosh barukh Hu y'malei rachamim aleihem, l'hachalimam
u-l'rapotam u-l'hachazikam, v'yishlach lahem m'heirah r'fuah sh'leimah min ha-shamayim,
r'fuat ha-nefesh u-r'fuat ha-guf, hashta ba'agalah u-vizman kariv. V'nomar: Amein.*

Oh God, from You comes the whole world. You blessed our fathers and
mothers from old times, Sarah and Abraham, Rebecca and Isaac, Rachel and
Leah and Jacob, with health and strength. And now we ask that You bless
these, the ones we love, the ones who are sick. They need strength and
health, too. Hold us all in Your hands, filling us with joy and wellness.

בָּרוּךְ אַתָּה יְיָ רוֹפֵא הַחוֹלִים.

Barukh Atah Adonai, rofei ha-cholim.

We praise You, the One who helps us heal the sick.

We Can Praise God
עָלֵינוּ

עָלֵינוּ לְשַׁבֵּחַ לַאֲדוֹן הַכֹּל, לָתֵת גְּדֻלָּה לְיוֹצֵר בְּרֵאשִׁית,
שֶׁלֹּא עָשָׂנוּ כְּגוֹיֵי הָאֲרָצוֹת, וְלֹא שָׂמָנוּ כְּמִשְׁפְּחוֹת הָאֲדָמָה;
שֶׁלֹּא שָׂם חֶלְקֵנוּ כָּהֶם, וְגוֹרָלֵנוּ כְּכָל הֲמוֹנָם.
וַאֲנַחְנוּ כּוֹרְעִים וּמִשְׁתַּחֲוִים וּמוֹדִים
לִפְנֵי מֶלֶךְ מַלְכֵי הַמְּלָכִים הַקָּדוֹשׁ בָּרוּךְ הוּא.

Aleinu l'sha-bei-ach la'adon hakol, lateit g'dula l'yotzer b'reishit,
shelo asanu k'goyei ha-aratzot, v'lo samanu k'mishhp'chot ha'adamah.
Shelo sam chelkenu kahem, v'goraleinu k'khol hamonam.
Va'anachnu kor'im umishtachavim umodim
Lifnei melekh malkhei ha-m'lakhim ha-kadosh barukh Hu.

We praise You, Adonai our God.
You are the Maker of skies and earth. You hold us in Your hand,
and teach us to do mitzvot to help all of humankind.
Therefore we praise You,
the Holy and Blessed One.

שֶׁהוּא נוֹטֶה שָׁמַיִם וְיוֹסֵד אָרֶץ, וּמוֹשַׁב יְקָרוֹ
בַּשָּׁמַיִם מִמַּעַל, וּשְׁכִנַת עֻזּוֹ בְּגָבְהֵי מְרוֹמִים.
הוּא אֱלֹהֵינוּ, אֵין עוֹד; אֱמֶת מַלְכֵּנוּ, אֶפֶס זוּלָתוֹ,
כַּכָּתוּב בְּתוֹרָתוֹ: וְיָדַעְתָּ הַיּוֹם וַהֲשֵׁבֹתָ
אֶל-לְבָבֶךָ, כִּי יְיָ הוּא הָאֱלֹהִים בַּשָּׁמַיִם מִמַּעַל
וְעַל-הָאָרֶץ מִתַּחַת, אֵין עוֹד.

Shehu noteh shamayim v'yoseid aretz, u-moshav y'karo bashamayim mima'al, u-sh'vinat uzo b'govhei m'romim. Hu Eloheinu ein od; emet Malkeinu, efes zulato, kakatuv b'torato: v'yada'ta hayom v'hasheivota el-l'vavekha, ki Adonai Hu ha-Elohim bashamayim mima'al v'al-ha-aretz mitachat, ein od.

Adonai you made the whole universe.
You sure are great!

וְנֶאֱמַר: וְהָיָה יהוה
לְמֶלֶךְ עַל-כָּל-הָאָרֶץ
בַּיּוֹם הַהוּא יִהְיֶה יהוה אֶחָד
וּשְׁמוֹ אֶחָד.

*Vene'emar: v'hayah Adonai l'melekh al kol ha'aretz,
Bayom ha-hu yih'yeh Adonai echad
u-sh'mo echad.*

Kaddish to Remember

קדיש יתום

Now is the time to remember. Who do we remember? We think about all those people whom we have loved who are not here with us any more, people who have died. When we think of them, indeed, we are sad. But we are oh, so thankful that they were in our lives, that we loved them and that they loved us. Let's remember them now.

יִתְגַּדַּל וְיִתְקַדַּשׁ שְׁמֵהּ רַבָּא בְּעָלְמָא דִּי-בְרָא כִרְעוּתֵהּ,

וְיַמְלִיךְ מַלְכוּתֵהּ בְּחַיֵּיכוֹן וּבְיוֹמֵיכוֹן וּבְחַיֵּי דְכָל-בֵּית יִשְׂרָאֵל,

בַּעֲגָלָא וּבִזְמַן קָרִיב וְאִמְרוּ אָמֵן.

יְהֵא שְׁמֵהּ רַבָּא מְבָרַךְ לְעָלַם וּלְעָלְמֵי עָלְמַיָּא.

יִתְבָּרַךְ וְיִשְׁתַּבַּח וְיִתְפָּאַר וְיִתְרוֹמַם וְיִתְנַשֵּׂא,

וְיִתְהַדַּר וְיִתְעַלֶּה וְיִתְהַלָּל שְׁמֵהּ דְּקוּדְשָׁא, בְּרִיךְ הוּא,

לְעֵלָּא מִן-כָּל-בִּרְכָתָא וְשִׁירָתָא,

תֻּשְׁבְּחָתָא וְנֶחֱמָתָא דַּאֲמִירָן בְּעָלְמָא, וְאִמְרוּ אָמֵן.

יְהֵא שְׁלָמָא רַבָּא מִן-שְׁמַיָּא וְחַיִּים עָלֵינוּ

וְעַל-כָּל-יִשְׂרָאֵל, וְאִמְרוּ אָמֵן.

עֹשֶׂה שָׁלוֹם בִּמְרוֹמָיו הוּא יַעֲשֶׂה שָׁלוֹם עָלֵינוּ

וְעַל-כָּל-יִשְׂרָאֵל,

וְאִמְרוּ אָמֵן.

Yitgadal v'yitkadash sh'mei raba b'alma div'ra khirutei
v'yamlikh malkhutei b'chayeikhon u-v'yomeikhon u-v'chayei d'khol beit yisrael,
ba'agalah u-vizman kariv v'imru amein.
Y'hei sh'mei raba m'vorakh l'olam ul'al'mei almaya.
Yitbarakh v'yishtabakh v'yitpa'ar v'yitromam v'yitnasei
v'yit'hadar v'yitaleh v'yit'halal sh'mei d'kudesha, b'rikh hu,
l'eila min kol bir'khatah v'shirata
tush'b'chatah v'nechemata da'a'miran b'alma v'imru amen.
Y'hei sh'lama raba min sh'maya v'chayim aleinu v'al kol yisrael, vimru amein.
Oseh shalom bimromav hu ya'aseh shalom, aleinu v'al kol yisrael, v'imru amein.

God has made a great world.
We praise You, Adonai and thank You
for all that we have:
for our families, and our friends;
for all of those
who have lived before us
and who have made it possible
for us to be alive today!
And we hope that, with our help,
peace will come to us all.

Family Blessings
ברכות המשפחה

For a boy:

יְשִׂימְךָ אֱלֹהִים כְּאֶפְרַיִם וְכִמְנַשֶּׁה.

Y'simkha Elohim k'efrayim v'khimenasheh.

May God lead you to be like Ephraim and Manasseh.

For a girl:

יְשִׂימֵךְ אֱלֹהִים כְּשָׂרָה, כְּרִבְקָה, כְּרָחֵל, וּכְלֵאָה.

Y'simeikh Elohim k'sarah, k'rivkah, k'racheil, u-kh'leiah.

May God lead you to be like Sarah, Rebecca, Rachel, and Leah.

For everyone:

יְבָרֶכְךָ יְיָ וְיִשְׁמְרֶךָ.
יָאֵר יְיָ פָּנָיו אֵלֶיךָ וִיחֻנֶּךָּ.
יִשָּׂא יְיָ פָּנָיו אֵלֶיךָ וְיָשֵׂם לְךָ שָׁלוֹם.

Y'varekh'kha Adonai v'yish'm'rekha.
Ya'eir Adonai panav eilekha vichunekha.
Yisa Adonai panav eilekha v'yaseim l'kha shalom.

May God bless you and protect you.

May God's light shine on you, and may God be kind to you.

May God always be present with you, and give you peace.

Kiddush for Erev Shabbat

קדוש

בָּרוּךְ אַתָּה, יְיָ אֱלֹהֵינוּ, מֶלֶךְ הָעוֹלָם, בּוֹרֵא פְּרִי הַגָּפֶן.

Barukh Atah, Adonai Eloheinu, Melekh ha-olam, borei p'ri ha-gafen.

You are a wonder, Adonai, and we thank you for the grapes that grow on vines, just right to squeeze into sweet juice for us to drink.

בָּרוּךְ אַתָּה, יְיָ אֱלֹהֵינוּ, מֶלֶךְ הָעוֹלָם, אֲשֶׁר קִדְּשָׁנוּ
בְּמִצְוֹתָיו וְרָצָה בָנוּ, וְשַׁבָּת קָדְשׁוֹ בְּאַהֲבָה וּבְרָצוֹן הִנְחִילָנוּ,
זִכָּרוֹן לְמַעֲשֵׂה בְרֵאשִׁית. כִּי הוּא יוֹם תְּחִלָּה לְמִקְרָאֵי קֹדֶשׁ,
זֵכֶר לִיצִיאַת מִצְרָיִם. כִּי בָנוּ בָחַרְתָּ, וְאוֹתָנוּ קִדַּשְׁתָּ מִכָּל
הָעַמִּים. וְשַׁבָּת קָדְשְׁךָ בְּאַהֲבָה וּבְרָצוֹן הִנְחַלְתָּנוּ.
בָּרוּךְ אַתָּה, יְיָ, מְקַדֵּשׁ הַשַּׁבָּת.

Barukh Atah, Adonai Eloheinu, Melekh ha-olam, asher kid'shanu b'mitzvotav v'ratzah vanu, v'Shabbat kodsho b'ahavah u-v'ratzon hinchilanu, zikaron l'ma-aseh v'reishit. Ki hu yom t'chilah l'mikra-ei kodesh, zekher litziat Mitzrayim. Ki vanu vacharta, v'otanu kidashta mikol ha-amim. V'Shabbat kodsh'kha b'ahavah uv-ratzon hinchaltanu. Barukh Atah, Adonai, m'kadeish ha-Shabbat.

Ha-Motzi

המוציא

בָּרוּךְ אַתָּה, יְיָ אֱלֹהֵינוּ, מֶלֶךְ הָעוֹלָם, הַמּוֹצִיא לֶחֶם מִן הָאָרֶץ.

Barukh Atah, Adonai Eloheinu, Melekh ha-olam, ha-motzi lechem min ha-aretz.

We are in wonder, Adonai, because from a tiny seed, full of God-given life, stalks of wheat grow, and then we make the wheat into challah. We thank You, Adonai.

Acknowledgments

Congregation Kol Ami and the Jewish Community School,
Elmira, New York, provided the opportunity to develop this book.

The photograph on page 13 is courtesy of
Temple Emanuel, Greensboro, North Carolina.

We thank Sharon Shafrir for proofreading this edition.

The Hebrew text is set in Adobe Hebrew, commissioned from Tiro Typeworks and designed by John Hudson in 2004–05. The proportions are based on those of traditional Sefardic formal book hands. The low contrast and dynamic balancing of the letterforms help to facilitate reading and to differentiate similar characters.

The English text is set in Maiandra GD, designed by Dennis Pasternak for the Galápagos Design Group in 1994. It was inspired by Oswald Bruce Cooper's hand lettering for an advertisement in 1909. Influenced by Greek inscriptions, it has been redrawn for extended text use.

I0086864

www.ingramcontent.com/pod-product-compliance
Lightning Source LLC
Chambersburg PA
CBHW041238040426
42445CB00004B/73

9 780615 977164